W a y f a r e r s

Katrinka Moore

Pelekinesis

ISBN-13: 978-1-938349-74-4
eISBN: 978-1-938349-75-1
Library of Congress Control Number: 2017942253

Excerpt from "Twelfth Morning; or What You Will" from POEMS by Elizabeth Bishop. Copyright © 2011 by The Alice H. Methfessel Trust. Reprinted by permission of Farrar, Straus and Giroux.

Excerpt from "Ode to the Road" from ALL THE ODES by Pablo Neruda, Edited by Ilan Stavans. Copyright © 2013 by Pablo Neruda and Fundación Pablo Neruda. Reprinted by permission of Farrar, Straus and Giroux

Cover artwork by Katrinka Moore
Layout and Book Design by Mark Givens
Copy editor: Cindy Hochman of "100 Proof" Copyediting Services

First Pelekinesis Printing 2018
For information:
Pelekinesis, 112 Harvard Ave #65, Claremont, CA 91711 USA

Pelekinesis
www.pelekinesis.com

for Michael

CONTENTS

Notes

Acknowledgments

Wayfarers

WHAT YOU WILL

The sea's off somewhere, doing nothing. Listen.
— Elizabeth Bishop

The mind's off somewhere, doing nothing. Listen,
humming to itself.

Off somewhere, doing something. Counts
elephants, waiting for thunder.

Elsewhere, nothing. Out to sea, coasting
on waves.

Rides the wing of a sandpiper, whole flock
swerving in harmony.

Certainly it swerves, the mind. Listen,
back from its travels, tales.

I THE ROLLING WORLD

*each path its own story, each
traveler with her own tale*

PARTING

We come to a crossing. Swallows
fly over, we hear an owl or
is it a dove, distant, auspices

we've lost the means to unravel.

Last leaves on bone-thin oak limbs, wind-
loosened, take wing — these cloud-birds
drift down around us, slow

as we are at parting.   Now   you
tack windward, I veer toward
the day-rising moon

(this light a gift dark at the edges).

Backs turned, we don't look round — already
dust washes over where we've been.
Our horses neigh to each other.

THE ROLLING WORLD

The fire burned for days and then the most bereaved
    rekindled it and camped in the ruins.
Others of us turned our backs, built our own fires.

The old woman remained, sleeping on fallen brick, eating, if
    she ate, from abandoned stores in shells of houses.
But I had my daughters, so I left her.
I looked back — the stay-behinds drifted, digging in the debris,
    carrying artifacts from one pile of rubble to another.

I was afraid, but I remembered how to find water, forage
    thistle and tuber my mother had shown me long ago,
    before we came to that place, before I settled there.
I was afraid, but I would not fall in with others from the city.
I took the children on paths I knew from my youth, then we
    quit those and forged our own way.

GEOMANCY

Astray in a wayward
    world   unsheltered, keep
an eye out for the yawning
      beneath   Stumble across
a signal, sound pulsing   Thirst
  bumps at your side   Stay
  or strike camp   settle
    or seek   This once-peopled
track   rank   shadowy
   secant cut through
    a bend in the trail
Moonlit circle   handful
    of thrown earth

LEONIDS

We woke without knowing.
A windless night, clear —
stars dove into the lake, hail-
heavy, blizzard-thick, trailing
white-hot streams. Fireballs
burst into colors, lit our up-
turned faces, while the fixed
stars above shone bright
as ever. And the sounds —
rustles like breeze-stirred
cattails, snaps like ice-
cracked limbs. We gazed
till daybreak, then combed
the shore for thunderstones.

ADRIFT

Nightfall, snow woods, abandoned
cabin — behind the shoved-open
door, echoes shimmy.

Earth-caught, we surrender chaos
to chance, to grace

huddle inside empty
shelter, cold and dirty, a hub
with spokes stretching
far into darkness.

Above the roof, the trees, calls
of night-flying birds.

Dawn, we clamber
out, worn hull, jangled core

sweet air   daylight
the rolling world.

COSMOGONY

I'd been cast out, into
    silence and solitude, caught

between all that might happen
    and what comes into being.

Traveled through stillness
    through soundless stirring

chanced upon denizens
    in an abraded world, sitting

beside open fires. *Wait,*
    eyes open: A gathering

of elements, entangled, burst
    apart, flew asunder — radiated —

shifting center, periphery. We
    scoured for remnants, then

clustered to enter
    the unfolding.

RIVERBANK

At dusk they climb down
from the ridge, slope dense
with goat's-thorn, and lie
on a low sandy bank. Across

the river limestone cliffs rise
straight out of the water. A bad
place to sleep if rain comes but
they are tired, do not think. Deep

night they wake, cliffs on fire —
conflagration, searchlights? *Stay
still.* Full moon lifts above the ridge,
white-gold, illuminates limestone, glow

spilling over the wayfarers. Beyond,
somewhere, arpeggio of howls.

DARKLING

Days later, still dust-thick air, haze-fraught, overgrown
path bound by forest, she strides, sun-longing —

what ground gained, how far to go, idle
to imagine, landmarks awry.

She presses on, unflinching, faltering, stumbles
on last-glow goldenrod, hears music —

mountain-caught cloud, yellow
birds sing in dark daylight.

SORTIE

By great luck we found our horses amidst the herd
of feral mares, and leaping on we guided them
with our knees, the way we'd learned as children
before we were allowed the use of bridles.

The wild ones shied but let us ride among them
and that is how we escaped, leaning low
on our horses' necks so the herders —
kidnappers, bandits — did not see us.

    fear-sweat   dry mouth
    damp hair   warm companion

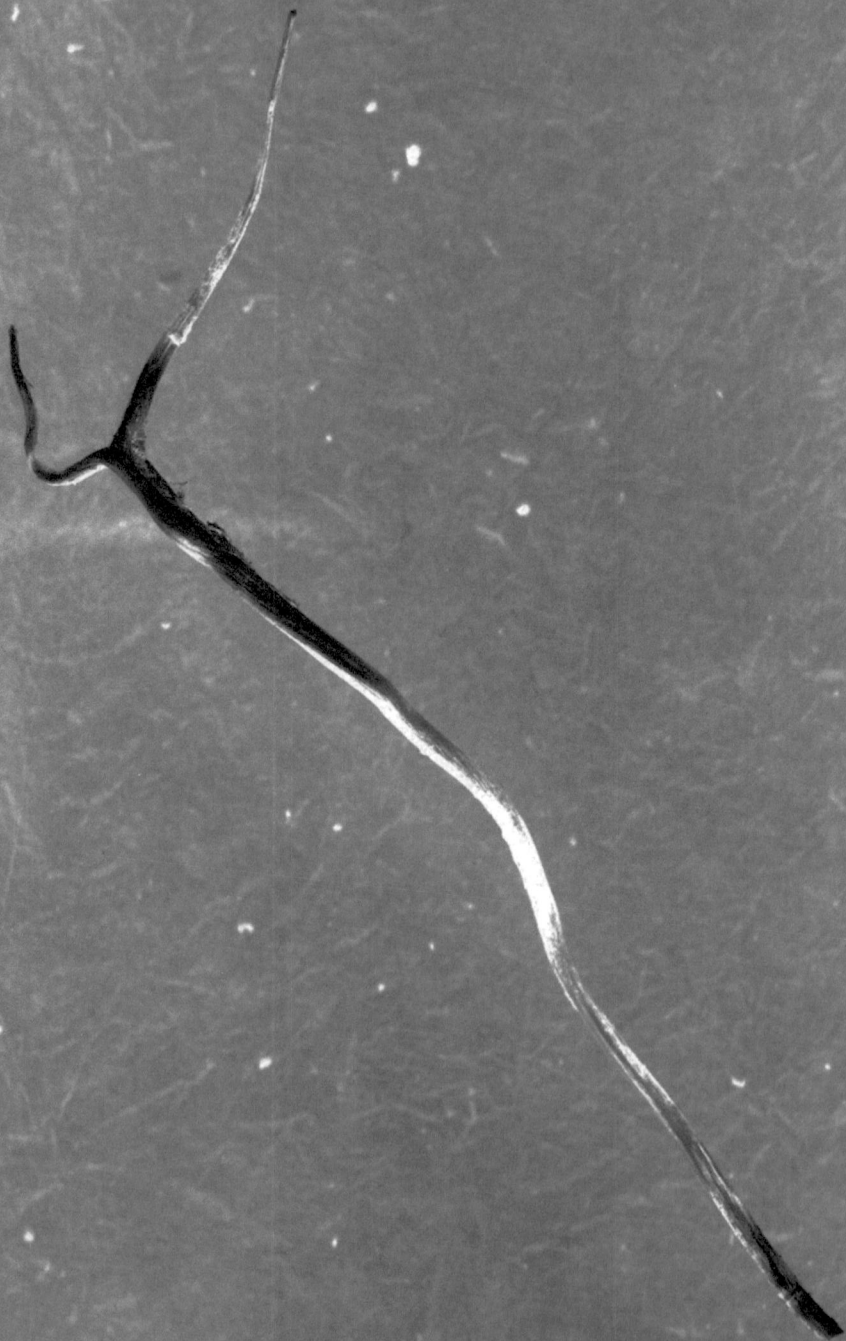

DIVINATION

Before they leave
the woodlands she cuts a forked
stick, witch hazel

ties it to her pack.
Now on the high plains she takes
it out, holds

a prong in each hand
paces, waits for the vertex lightning-
like to dip or twist —

pools of water
inside the earth, silent
as ice.

KATABASIS

Tunnel of shrub and vine
hems in the summer-dry stream
steamy thread — I duck in
follow the channel, Stygian.

Knees bent, back hunched,
Kokopelli with damp hair
for feathers, head down, eyes
on the bed of bare stones

where a clear pool survives —
ocher sand-and-pebble bottom
strider bugs on the rim, their great-
wheeled shadows roll below.

Haze-filtered sunlight — leaves and sky
fill the puddle, deep as the ocean.

ASCENT

Ancient shore, sand
stirred by incoming
tide, turned to stone

How your feet feel
on this ledge, its
rippled face, how air

touches your skin, how
light from all sides
reaches your eyes

THINGS SO LIGHT THEY FIND THE ACT OF FALLING HEAVY GOING

On yellow wings too light to touch down
a swallowtail crosses the sun-shining river —
her wavy path, tiny ups and downs.
Yellow wings too light to touch down
most of her life spent far-shore bound.
What's over there that she can't find here?
On yellow wings too light to touch down
she crosses, unswallowed, the sun-shining river.

OVERLAND

Island of lava, rain springs
out of every crevice
reckless water-courses.

Flocks of light, thickets
of the season, whid
of unnamed creatures.

Basaltic plateau —
a rider gallops
into the trade wind, misses
the track and so finds
this jumbled village, rill
over rock, over ruins.

Children round up
cries rich and harsh
as fast as the ponies will run.

TANGENT

Sidetracking as an art — veer
wander   meander

Step off the trail, lost
way-seek, stray further

Pause on a point
of a circle

(one of many around
where you mean to return)

Now this point's the center
Orbits ripple out, overlap

AWAY

She scrambles up wooded slopes
rock-slippery, reaches an archaic
crater open to the sky — now

fertile earth, pasture
for dairy cows ringing
as they graze — at heart

a medieval chapel, worn
stone walls, dung in the yard,
tiles torn from the roof

slender apse window
that lets light barely in,
tiny altar, nowhere to hide.

She sees an iron rod, bars
the door, bell-haunted
sanctuary   or   sepulcher.

WE COME TO A RIVER

River so wide waves
nuzzle the bank, white foam
in the distance, pelicans
diving, so deep we can't
wade, so rough we can't
swim to that far-off shore.

Here a calm inlet, shallow,
wild iris — through moss-
dangling cypress we hear
a slow wing-beat, glimpse
a pair of bald eagles.

A moccasin hovers, head
at the surface like a nub
of new bulrush, peril bides
as water laps and subsides.

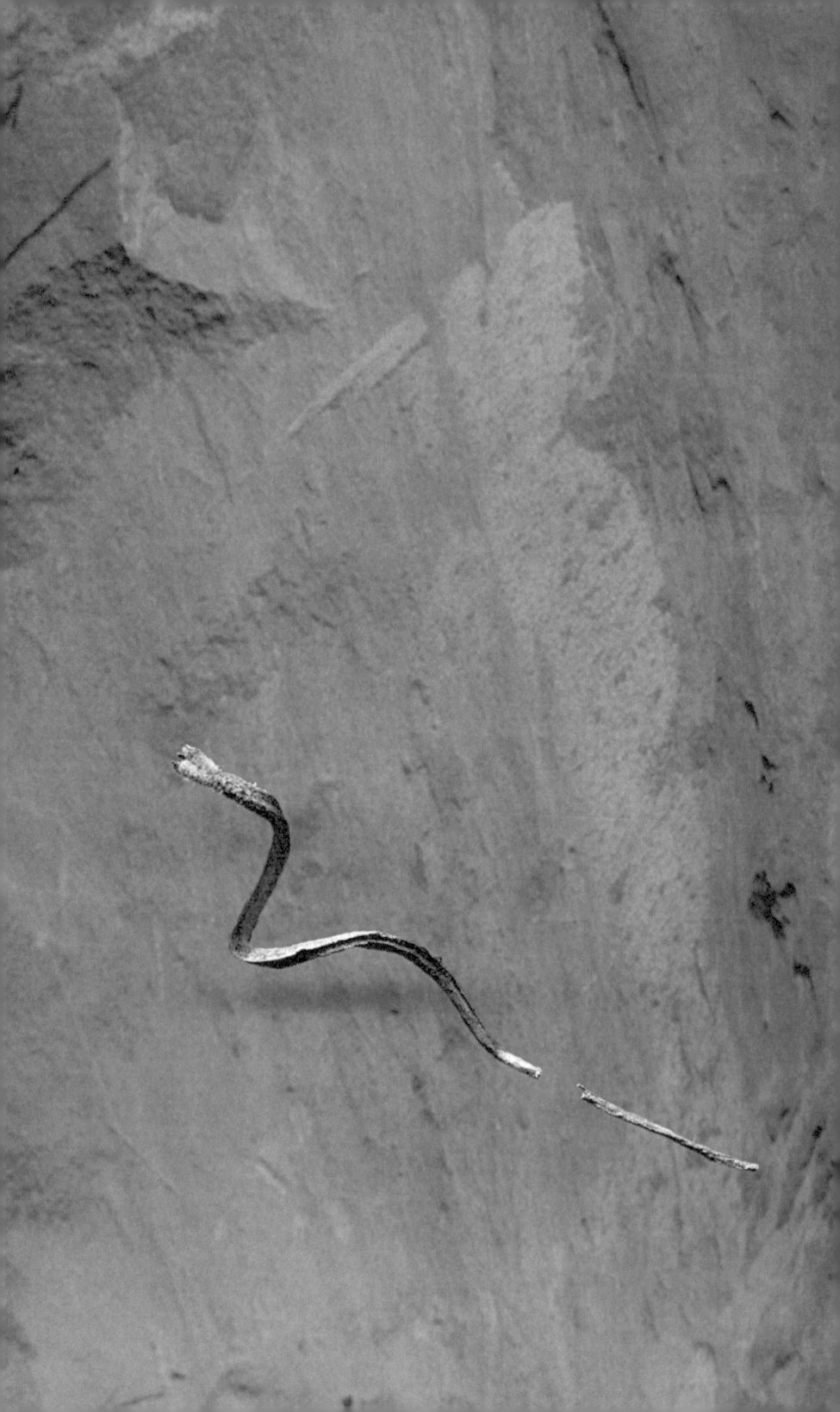

SERPENTINA

Gorge means throat and the rovers falter
at the sheer walls, narrow floor, wonder

if it is a path, wonder where it leads — horseshoe
curve to the right, straightaway, bend to the left.

Down here winding, neither of them knows
which direction they're walking, yesterday's

clear sky turned thick-clouded, low over long-
empty channel, in this present no water, no sun, no

wind. Silence, or as close as they've ever been.

HUSH

over night ice
crusted the stream,
snared low-lying
limbs, caught cataract
as it fell, hushed
the din of rushing

        running

beneath translucent
rind dark knots
of water form
and shift amoeba-
like then burst
back into down-
ward scramble

WASH

wind-warped cedar, rock and stone
heat and the glare of it

        sheds as she goes, grows gaunt

a single willow where water once ran

        hunkers down, heels
        sink in soft soil

shade, trace of damp air

        walks on for the sake of it

twist in the trail, rise

LUNA LURA

Drawn by this wanderer
where light falls softly, flows
over its rough face, swells,
dissolves, begins again.

We circle, flutter, romp,
sleep in crevices, bask
in radiance. Come.

II   A CROSSING

After the Great War,
her husband came home
and they headed west
with their young son.

CROW

Her mother left behind, the
river. A thousand miles
of dusty road. A crow
blocks the way, eating
carrion. They pull around,
crush a prickly pear. She
knows to throw spilled salt,
knock on wood, but how
to stave off this dark sign?

Empty space left ajar, sliver
in the margins.

THE ISLE IS FULL OF NOISES

Not isle — it's more akin
to ocean, Ariel's sea
change, song of bones —

wheels rubbing on rough
road, motor's roar, wind-
rush in their ears —

songs of the living —
whip-poor-will, roadrunner's
rattle, howls and barks of

unseen creatures, descant
to the outside-of-time silence
from before life arrived

with its noises, music, words.
She thinks of her grandfather
sitting on the sunny side

of the house, ancient, blind. She
read to him, retired magician —
sometimes he'd speak a line

before she reached it, sometimes
he'd wait to hear it.

SEA ROAD

Ocher undulations
on both sides
from the road
toward a far-flung
they are traveling
they are crossing
sea-worthy vessel.
docked, she sees
unveil its elements:
spines on prickly
in the sand. In
blossoms. The boy

spill over
roll away
wave unceasing
shore. She thinks
through a shallow ocean
brine in a barely
Pulled over, briefly
the dun-colored sameness
openings in ocotillo,
pear, speckled pebbles
stillness the landscape
finds a sea shell.

WIND ROAD

Ungarnished sky curves overhead but near the horizon
fast-flowing clouds stutter sunlight on faint mountains.

From high and far away wind swoops earthward
at dusk, sand-stirring as they make camp, ring
of light bound by the dark.

She stands to breast the tide. It streams through
her skin, enters her bones, rides with her blood. She's
a hoodoo, windswept, casting off sediment —

MIDDAY

A dry shining
stifles sound, smothers
motion. They're lulled —

even the boy — resting
under a cloth stretched
tent-like for shade. No

calls, no cries, no buzzes,
no slithers, no scampers, no
wings beating. Fettered

by stillness — siesta
over, time to move
on — they don't stir.

GILA

Already the boy's
forgotten the Concho
back home, greener terrain.

Already he lives only
in desert, so he falls for
the Gila, shallow but flowing —

bankside cottonwood,
another family — roasting
cabrito — children are wading.

He careens toward the others,
ignoring his mother, stumbles
and falls, chortles, hops up —

Old, he feels the splash of cold
water, hears the girls' shrieks
the boys' laughter. Old-in-his-chair

he smells the goat on the spit
sees the smooth white stones
in the riverbed.

ROUND

the dark pales, then
a red seam opens the rim
and headlong settles into unrelenting

radiance, sealed by another red line,
black izle-filled sky, some-
times moonlight

days and nights, this crossing

||| DWELLING

Ay traveler!
You don't go and don't return:
you are
made of roads

— PABLO NERUDA

MEASURE

Waves of milkweed, unbridled
grass, winged humming. We

take hands and run overland, last
light of a summer day. Field

mouse rides in hawk's talons,
brief bird's-eye view of home.

Inchworm, navigating without
a rhumb line. A bumblebee

burrows. Somebody's
got to chart all that space.

TURN

Gray windy autumn — yellow
and red drift like snow. Pitch
green of hemlock, white wing
of owl. How to turn away, out-
side, away from a landscape.
Deep night, a varmint piles
leaves inside the bedroom
wall. Tiny claws scurry
across an attic beam. The last
migrating birds left days
ago. Mouse means to stay.

GRAVITATION

Two cars, still distant,
drive toward the same span

of road — a one-lane
bridge, wood-slat base,

railing askew. Below, a
low-running creek, slow

and muddy, gumbo, and on
the banks, weedy bamboo. Waves

weight   force   mass
field   acceleration

A boy leans on the rail,
watches a pig-tailed girl

wade through the water, get
waylaid, caught, stuck — run

lopsided home, boot
sock, boot sock.

SOUND OF WATER

Each phase of the moon
a surprise, appearing
between bouts of rough
weather. She sloshes

through the wet field, hears
a frog plop in a puddle
behind her. Ungathered
thoughts in cloudy light.

Steps onto a log, trips over a turtle
lodged at the far end, snapping,
ankylosauran. Arms splay,
she topples, splatters mud.

Ancient watery world. Looks
for the frog in its *warm little pond.*
Thunder, still distant, pitches in. Our
earliest kin, muck and lightning.

RENISH

Sits with the forest
at her back, sunlight
that slips between

leaves swallowed
by thick black
fur. Watches, eyes

veiled. Ambles
silently over up-
rooted trees, downed

limbs. An obsolete
word of unknown
origin: *wild, strange*

DWELLING

word-stealing quiet   hidden

strata   half-thought words

feather-light bones   riffled

feathers left behind   relics

land-bound leaves   unbound

air-caught   lift   linger

slow-gathering color   fade-

away   stars' slow circle

thief-moon's light   shadow

throwing   dark become light

HOUSE, BIRD

Sometimes, riding our bikes on rutted
shell roads, past creeks and pastures,
we'd light on an abandoned house —
overgrown driveway, roof sagging, porch
fallen in — and wander through, window glass
on the floor, darkness behind torn wallpaper.

Once, we pushed open a front door and heard
singing and clicking. We crept from room
to room, rusty nail-points, cracked beams,
trying to reach the bird, catch its sounds.

FIELD

Sideshadow nudges
periphery, flutters
the ground, flickers
the sapling.

This fox-thing trots
beside us, just
behind. Corner
of the eye.

Stop short, spin
around — catch
nothing-in-air.

Yarrows stir, fire-
weed wavers.

~ ~ ~

See the abandoned
field turn slowly back
to forest. See it change
from light to shadow to
light throughout the day. Come
clouds, come cloud-erasing wind.

CELEBRATE

summer-still, then night wind sweeps
in bearing clouds that crowd the day-
long sky and sunlight (water-like) finds
a path downward, a few rays, short-living
glint on the landscape, windblown

borderland where air empties one being
into another, wears away edges till
everything bumps up together, what a place,
transitory, what better way to celebrate than
to leave off being separate for a while, revel

in this *spotted World*, our brush against it lucky
despite the flaws — *sufficient unto the day*
though the first part's more fun, taking
no thought for the morrow

BONE-HOUSE SONG

What's all this juice and all this joy
bounding spirit in the bone-house?
Where from and bound, I wonder, where?
What's all this joy and all this juice?
Give beauty back, beauty, beauty
share life as life does air.
All this — this juice, this joy — unbinds
the spirit in the bone-house.

WHEN SHE DIVES

water waves mute   sound waves and

she drifts through   silent sun rays

refracted, misty   her hair unspools

slow-flapping   wings

light body buoys skyward   gravity

draws bottomward   she hovers   floats

in mote-filled quiet   going nowhere

yields   kicks   rises   breathes

awash in air   she listens

BONE POND

Dark clouds, but for now
the scow scoots over water
lilies, flat bottom tickled,
glides toward a half-sunk
log, bare gangly limbs.

Bare limbs, barkless
trunks, soaked roots,
lakeside dead oaks
stretch toward clouds
scooting through the sky.

Sky in the water, lilies
the sun. Gangly stems
stretch toward the bottom
mucky, yawning, so deep
nothing you see can reach it.

I reach for the oars —
the scow scoots into shallow
water, gets caught on the log,
trapped in its limbs. The lilies
are tickled. Dark clouds loom.

COWARTS CREEK

wind circles the house
rain stipples the roof
creek meanders behind
the ramshackle house

   wind ferrets out flaws
   prods unputtied windows
   jars loose-fitting doors

      rain pummels the roof
      batters breaches from blown-
      away shingles

        creek rushes, it reaches
        past banks, over levee

          wind tears around rooms
          rain pierces the ceiling
          creek courses beneath
          the ramshackle house on blocks

~   ~   ~

swish against bedpost, black behind windows
her feet reach the ankle-deep floor
drought in her childhood, all of them
wishing for rain
creek in the house, swallowing years

she wades to the kitchen, clambers
onto the counter, waits without knowing
grass outside waving beneath
how high on the oaks, she'd wanted to live
among trees

hears a motor, a shout, her neighbors, their outboard
away in the watery world
in the wind in the rain

REMNANTS

torn tip of a butterfly
wing   edge of a page ripped

from a manuscript   wind-
caught   half-heard lyrics

abraded frescoes   acrobats
and dolphins exuberant

on an earthquake island   allure
and ache of art   shards

on the floor   palaces built
over ruins   a thought the mind

skirts   door sagging   (lift
and shove)   window with

a broken sash   who stuck in
the dictionary to prop it up

LIMINAL

Somewhere between, a mucky
patch at the back steps, boot
prints stamped and stamped
over, sludge-filled tracks. Unruly
weather, toppled trunks, torn
wings, dangling roots. Mostly mud
and old snow but this morning
the field ice-glows in sunlight

bare and abundant. On one side
snowfall, on the other slow-opening
spring. Come evening I stand
in the doorway, kitchen warm
at my back. Boundless — something —
in every direction, darkness, sparks.

NIGHT CREATURES

Field stretches up to the woods. There's a sort
of path here, on the periphery, summer
evening, rose-tinted near-dark sky.

I turn away from the light, peer inside. Boulders and
oaks grow together, ferns and witch hazel
intertwine, intricate, indistinct.

A few steps into the woods, not far, I stand
still, fade out of color, lose angles, lines,
dissolve into smoke of a fire
gone out, hidden.

Small owl lands on a branch
near my head, we don't move, I
don't want her to fly. Under her eyes
I become material again, substantial. She
waits for me to go so she can get what she came for.

FALLING, SOMETIMES

When I fall asleep rain is hitting the roof,
steady as in childhood. Later I wake
to silence, watch the cloud-dusted
moon inch along its path.

> The creek behind my parents' house,
> bend of it, curling around us. I'd climb
> a live oak, settle in trunk-and-branch *V*.

What's the last sound of evening
before the first night noise? Day, dusk,
dusk, darkness. Waiting for stars to show.

Falling, sometimes, I'd let my body
slip between, not try to catch
on limbs, soft when I landed.

> When I got home she was gone
> already, always be sorry, her body
> a husk in familiar form, spirit
> scattered I thought, but dark
> before sunrise a dense shadow
> floated above me, mother-in-air.

GRACE

A fallow afternoon, hot,
slow clouds, unruffled
pond. Bird calls circle
outside of harmony, over-
lap, interlace. Sometimes
a solitary song slips
through. Grace

unweighed, porous and
buoyant (birds' airy
bones). Uncalled, comes
anyway. The voices fall

off and there's only
a hum, so soft we hear
it as silence. But that
happens after.

SCATTER

Some say the soul's a ghost,
immortal, immaterial. Lucretius

claims it's particles, scattered
throughout the body, gathered

into blood and bone, the visceral,
and like the flesh, ephemeral.

My mother's ashes blow across
the caldera, the sunlit grass.

Some feel the world's cold weight
some find its light.

Our home's a given-up-on farm, stone
walls that slump, fields growing trees, no

neighbors near, but city lights far off
are strong enough to crowd out stars

the ones we see a smattering
of those the farmer knew.

The boy bounds out, the screen
door slams and finches fly, some

settle in the pine, some soar so high we
watch, hands shading eyes, till all are gone.

NOTES

"What You Will": The epigraph is a line from Elizabeth Bishop's "Twelfth Morning; or What You Will."

"Parting": The last line is from "Taking Leave of a Friend," by Li Po (Li Bai), tr. by Ezra Pound.

"Leonids" was inspired by observers' accounts of the Leonids meteor shower in 1833. *Thunderstones* was a term for meteorites.

"Katabasis": The title means a descent (ancient Greek: *kata* down, *basis* going), such as a hero's journey to the underworld or a trip from the interior to the coast. Kokopelli is a humpbacked, flute-playing deity of Southwestern Native American lore.

"Things so light they find the act of falling heavy going": The title is
   from Book III of Lucretius' *The Nature of Things*, tr. by A.E.
   Stallings.

"The isle is full of noises": The title is from Shakespeare's *The Tempest*.

"Round": *Izle* means spark.

III Dwelling: The epigraph is from Pablo Neruda's "Ode to the
   Road," tr. by Ilan Stavans in *All the Odes*.

"Sound of Water": The title is from Basho's frog haiku, translated
   by Lafcadio Hearn. The phrase *warm little pond* is from
   Charles Darwin's letter to J.D. Hooker, 1871.

"Celebrate": The italicized *spotted World* is from Emily Dickinson's
   "When we stand on the tops of Things." The italicized phrases
   in the last two lines are from Matthew 6:34.

"Bone-house Song": The lines are from poems by Gerard Manley
   Hopkins.

ACKNOWLEDGMENTS

Grateful acknowledgment is made to the following publications, in which these poems, sometimes in earlier versions, first appeared:

Dos Gatos Press, *Weaving the Terrain:* "*The isle is full of noises,*" "Wind Road," "Midday," "Gila"

Ducts: "Gravitation," "Turn," "Falling, sometimes," "Night Creatures"

First Literary Review-East: "Leonids," "Overland," "Dwelling"

5_trope: "Measure," "Geomancy"

The Found Poetry Review: "Bone-house Song"

Möbius, The Poetry Magazine: "Hush"

Mom Egg Review: "Crow"

MungBeing: "Parting," "Darkling," "Cosmogony," "Sortie,"
    "Away," "Luna Lura," "Celebrate"

Otoliths: "What You Will," "Ascent," "Tangent," "Round,"
    "Renish," "Field," "When she dives"; artwork accompanying
    "The Rolling World," "Riverbank," "Renish."

Paulinskill Poetry Project, *Voices from Here, Vol. II:* "Grace,"
    "Scatter"

Snorkel: "Serpentina," "Wash"

The Stillwater Review: "House, bird," "Liminal"

The Woven Tale Press: "Riverbank," "Remnants"

Many thanks to Maura Candela, Linda Miller, and Elizabeth
Poreba for their insightful manuscript readings and to the
One O'clock Poets, the Evergreen Poets Workshop, and the
Rensselaerville Library Poetry Group for comments on many
of the poems in this book. Thanks also to Jamie Lawrence and
Robert Vizzini. I'm very grateful to Mark Givens of Pelekinesis
for his generosity and support.

ABOUT THE AUTHOR

Katrinka Moore started out in dance and choreography, made a brief foray into performance art, then shifted to poetry, eventually bringing visual components into her work. She is the author of three previous books, *Numa*, *Thief*, and *This is Not a Story*, winner of the New Women's Voices Prize. Moore grew up in rural Texas and now lives in New York.